Eager Street Academy #884
401 East Eager Street
Baltimore, MD 21202

ARCTIC THAW

ARCTIC

THAW

CLIMATE CHANGE and the
GLOBAL RACE for ENERGY RESOURCES

STEPHANIE SAMMARTINO MCPHERSON

TWENTY-FIRST CENTURY BOOKS
MINNEAPOLIS

For my father, ANGELO SAMMARTINO, with
thanks for his wisdom and inspiration, and in
memory of my mother, MARION SAMMARTINO,
a gifted writer, artist, and my best friend

The author wishes to thank Amy Fitzgerald and Domenica Di Piazza for
outstanding and invaluable editorial guidance, Edward Itta for sharing his hopes
and fears for the Arctic, and Richard McPherson for his unfailing encouragement.

Twenty-First Century Books
A division of Lerner Publishing Group, Inc.
241 First Avenue North
Minneapolis, MN 55401 USA

For updated reading levels and more information,
look up this title at www.lernerbooks.com.

Main body text set in ITC Esprit Std Book 10.5/15
Typeface provided by Adobe Systems

Library of Congress Cataloging-in-Publication Data

McPherson, Stephanie Sammartino.
Arctic thaw: Climate change and the global race for energy resources /
by Stephanie Sammartino McPherson.
pages cm
Includes bibliographical references and index.
ISBN 978–1–4677–2043–4 (library binding : alkaline paper)
ISBN 978–1–4677–4788–2 (EB pdf)
1. Global warming—Arctic regions—Juvenile literature. 2. Global
warming—Political aspects—Arctic regions—Juvenile literature. 3. Global
warming—Economic aspects—Arctic regions—Juvenile literature. 4.
Natural resources—Arctic regions—Juvenile literature. 5. Power resources—
Arctic regions—Juvenile literature. 6. Economic development—Arctic
regions—Juvenile literature. 7. International relations—Juvenile literature.
8. International economic relations—Juvenile literature. I. Title.
QC981.8.G56M395 2015
333.790911'3—dc23   2013025164

Manufactured in the United States of America
2 – VP – 5/1/15

CONTENTS

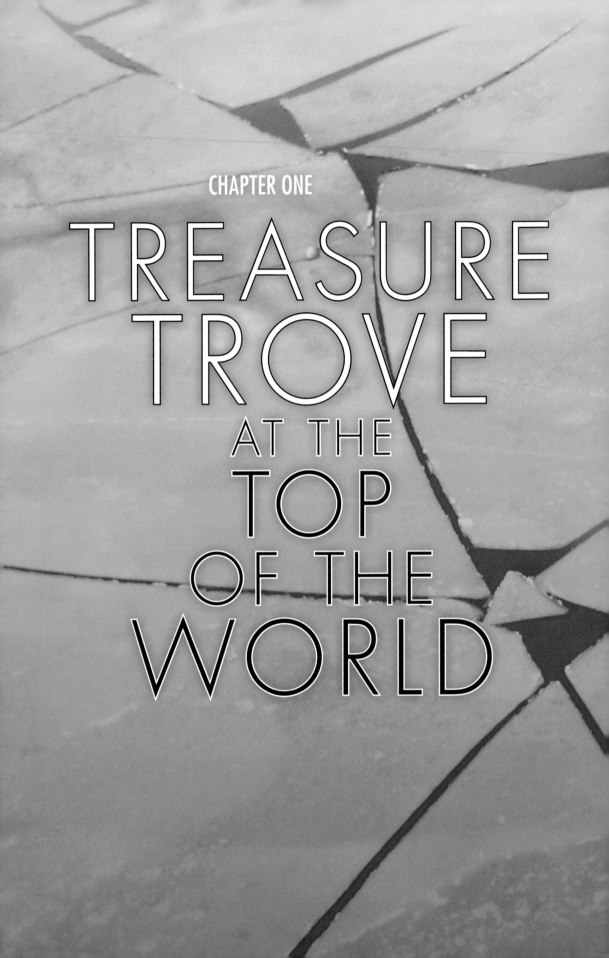

CHAPTER ONE

TREASURE TROVE

AT THE
TOP
OF THE
WORLD

TRAPPED BENEATH A LAYER OF THICK ARCTIC ICE, THE CREW OF THE RUSSIAN SUBMERSIBLE FACED A DESPERATE SITUATION. Their vessel, *Mir II*, held a limited supply of air. Time was running out for them to make it to the surface of the water. For more than an hour, the three men in *Mir II* searched for a break in the ice, wondering if they would come out alive.

All along, their mission had been fraught with danger. It began in late July 2007 as a two-ship expedition to the North Pole. The first ship, a state-of-the-art icebreaker, ground its way through the ice, opening a path for a research vessel to follow. "It took us seven days and seven nights to reach the North Pole," sixty-seven-year-old Russian diplomat and explorer Artur Chilingarov later said. "The ice was heavy. It was not a simple task."

But the Russian crew aimed to do more than cross the pole. They planned to touch the ground—a goal more difficult than it sounds. There is no landmass at the North Pole as there is in the southern continent of Antarctica. To reach solid earth, the Russians sent two submersibles, *Mir I* and *Mir II*, to the ocean floor. The subs entered the frigid water through a break in the ice and descended for three hours.

More than 2 miles (3 kilometers) down, the small subs landed on a yellowish ocean floor that showed no signs of life. After Chilingarov's craft raked samples from the soft clay, it moved on until it was directly under the geographic North Pole. A robotic arm extended from the vessel and planted a Russian flag made of rustproof titanium in the seabed.

Tension mounted as the subs began their slow rise to the surface. The men knew the ice above them would have drifted while they explored the ocean floor. They could only hope to emerge somewhere near a patch of open water.

When their worst fears were realized, the crew had no choice but to remain calm and search for another hole in the ice. After a seemingly endless hour and a half, both subs finally emerged safely into open air.

A research vessel lowers the Russian submersible *Mir I* into Arctic waters in 2007. The North Pole's ice cover at the time of the Russian expedition was nearly 80 feet (24 meters) thick in places. The tiny subs were not strong enough to break through that covering, so they entered the ocean through natural gaps in the ice.

Back aboard the mother ship at last, the men were jubilant. "If a hundred or a thousand years from now someone goes down to where we were, they will see the Russian flag," Chilingarov said proudly.

INTERNATIONAL CONTROVERSY

That flag and Chilingarov's boast caused an uproar. "This isn't the fifteenth century," complained Canada's foreign minister, Peter MacKay. "You can't go around the world and just plant flags and say 'We're claiming this territory.'"

On behalf of the US State Department, deputy spokesman Tom Casey joined in the skepticism. "I'm not sure whether they [the Russians] put a metal flag, a rubber flag, or a bed sheet on the ocean floor. Either way, it doesn't have any legal standing or effect on this claim."

Unfazed, the Russians continued to celebrate. Chilingarov brushed off the international criticism. "If someone doesn't like this, let them go down themselves—and then try to put something there. Russia must win. Russia has what it takes to win. The Arctic has always been Russian."

Chilingarov's strong words added fuel to a controversy that is not likely to go away anytime soon. Once considered a land apart, a beautiful but barren wilderness far removed from the concerns of everyday life, the Arctic has recently become the focus of worldwide interest. "The Arctic belongs to all the people around the world," Chinese admiral Yin Zhuo asserted in 2010, "as no nation has sovereignty over it."

Although China lies thousands of miles from the North Pole, its interest in Arctic matters is as strong as Russia's. In May 2013, China was granted permanent observer status at the Arctic Council. Created in 1996, this international body deals with issues facing the countries that border the Arctic Ocean. The eight members, sometimes called the Arctic

Artur Chilingarov shows off a photograph of the Russian flag his team planted on the seabed of the North Pole. Chilingarov, already well known both as a scientific researcher and as a politician, shot to even greater fame after the 2007 North Pole expedition. He continues to spearhead Russian efforts to claim Arctic territory.

Eight, are Canada, the United States, Russia, Denmark (which includes Greenland, a large Arctic island), Norway, Finland, Iceland, and Sweden. But other nations far removed from the Arctic have eagerly sought a voice on the council. India, Italy, Japan, Singapore, and South Korea were confirmed as permanent observers at the same time as China. "Our policy is that the key to success is through international cooperation," said Sweden's foreign minister, Carl Bildt, "whether dealing with the many risks associated with a changing Arctic or the various new economic opportunities."

AN ABUNDANCE OF RESOURCES

Why is the Arctic suddenly the center of so much international attention? The short answer is that climate change is dramatically altering the

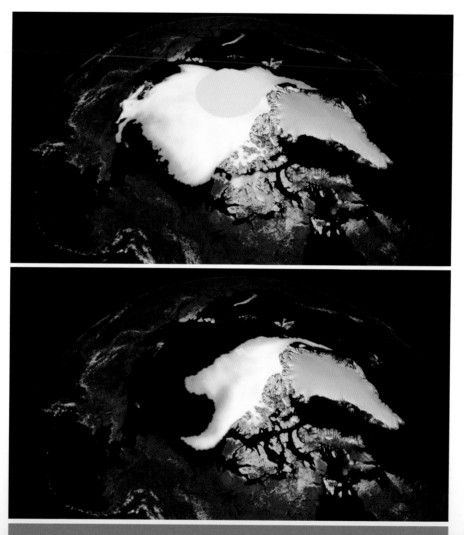

Since 1979 scientists have used satellites to monitor the amount of ice in the world's oceans. These satellite images show perennial ice cover—the sea ice that floats on the surface of the ocean and does not melt during the summer months—from 1980 *(top)* to 2012 *(bottom)*. As more and more ice melts each year over the summer and does not refreeze in the winter, perennial ice cover dwindles.

region's landscape, transforming it from an icebound frontier into a land of opportunity.

Over the past four decades, ice has diminished greatly due to climbing temperatures. One reason for this is that Arctic sea ice reflects as much as 90 percent of the sun's light and heat back into space. The dark waters left by melting ice do the opposite. They absorb most of the sun's heat and light. The warming of the water causes even more ice to melt.

As the Arctic continues to warm, new trade routes are opening across previously frozen waters. Many natural resources, formerly locked in the ice, are becoming available. Nations around the globe are determined to gain access to valuable metals, minerals, gems and, above all, the vast deposits of oil and natural gas beneath the Arctic Ocean.

Scientists believe the Arctic may hold about 13 percent of the world's undiscovered oil and 30 percent of its natural gas. These fossil fuels, formed over eons from the remains of ancient plants and animals, are humanity's most coveted energy sources. Crude oil pumped from the ground or the seabed is refined into fuel that heats homes and powers transportation all over the world. Smaller amounts of both crude oil and natural gas are used to generate electricity. Countries that do not have a sufficient supply of oil or natural gas must buy from those that do. Massive profits—and a sure source of energy—await anyone who can develop the Arctic's immense oil and gas deposits.

THE CANARY IN THE COAL MINE

Many experts fear that harvesting the Arctic's energy resources will come with a cost that cannot be measured in dollars and cents. The burning of oil, natural gas, and other fossil fuels releases carbon dioxide (CO_2) into the air. Carbon dioxide is a greenhouse gas that holds heat in Earth's atmosphere, preventing it from escaping into space. The more greenhouse gases in the atmosphere, the higher temperatures rise and the more drastically weather patterns shift. In the long run, developing the Arctic's fossil fuels for transportation and industry will cause even more greenhouse gases to be released, hastening climate change.

CLIMATE CHANGE is happening FASTER in the FAR NORTH than ANYWHERE ELSE ON EARTH.

Climate change is happening faster in the far north than anywhere else on Earth. As environmental scientist Howard Epstein warns, though, "What happens in the Arctic doesn't stay in the Arctic." For this reason, the Arctic is sometimes called the canary in the coal mine. Before the invention of gas-detecting equipment, miners carried canaries underground with them. If the air was dangerous to breathe, the canaries became ill before the humans did. A canary showing signs of stress or sickness served as a warning to the miners, who then exited the mine at once. Similarly, the Arctic thaw is a warning to the rest of the world. As the polar ice cap and sheets of land ice continue to melt, warmer temperatures, higher sea levels, and more extreme weather events can be expected all over the planet.

"GUARDIANS OF THE ARCTIC"

The indigenous peoples of the Arctic—many of whom are sometimes collectively known as the Inuit—are particularly affected by the changing

Large portions of Arctic glaciers melt in summertime. In recent years, less ice has refrozen in the winter, resulting in higher overall sea levels and shrinking ice cover. Remaining ice moves faster and breaks apart more easily.

weather and political claims. Thousands of years ago, their ancestors were the first to spot oil seeping up from the ground. Many follow a traditional way of life that is centuries older than the international community's growing interest in the region. Aqqaluk Lynge, former chairman of the Inuit Circumpolar Council (ICC), calls the indigenous peoples "the guardians of the Arctic." As such, they demand a say in how the region's newly accessible resources are used. In April 2009, the ICC issued a strongly worded Declaration on Arctic Sovereignty. The document states that industrial development in the Arctic is acceptable only if "it enhances the economic and social well-being of Inuit and safeguards our environmental security."

But with billions of dollars at stake, the Arctic is the scene of an ever-growing power struggle over energy resources. No one wants to be left out of the treasure trove at the top of the world. In the years to come, governments, multinational energy companies, and Arctic peoples will grapple with the challenge of developing Arctic resources without destroying the land, its inhabitants, and a unique way of life.

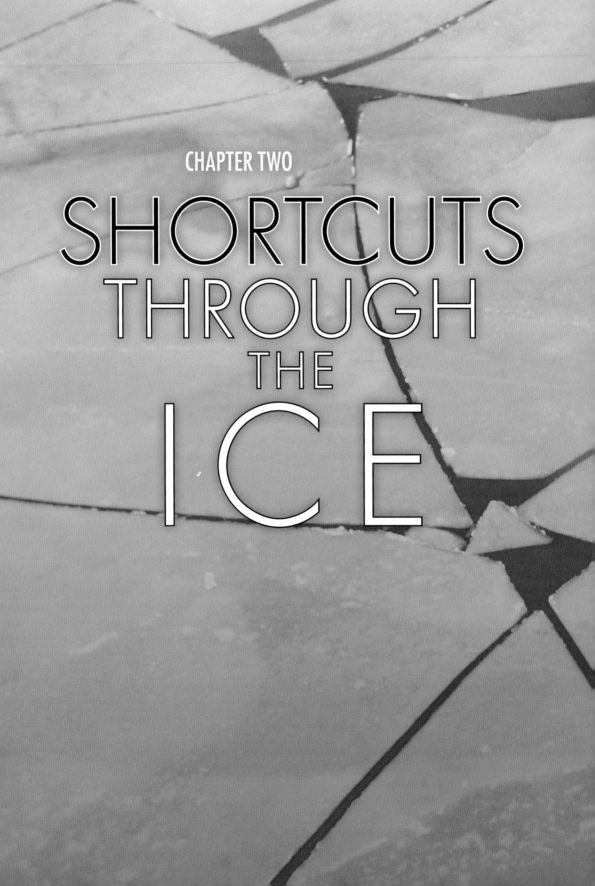

CHAPTER TWO

SHORTCUTS THROUGH THE ICE

IT WAS A LAST-MINUTE GAMBLE. When the cargo ship *Nordic Orion* arrived in Vancouver, Canada, on its way to Finland in September 2013, Arctic sea ice had shrunk to its summer low. The ship's owners made a bold decision. Instead of routing the ship south through the Panama Canal as scheduled, they would send it through the Northwest Passage. This fabled waterway, consisting of several channels through ice-choked islands, connects the North Atlantic and Pacific Oceans. Until the early 2000s, its icy pathways had been too treacherous for most ships to navigate even at the height of summer. But as a result of recent decreases in the amount of sea ice, the *Nordic Orion* had a shot at getting through.

Although its hull was strengthened to withstand sea ice, the Danish-owned carrier had no guarantee of a safe voyage. Icebergs and growlers—small, low-lying ice chunks that are hard to see—posed considerable risk. Icing, the freezing of sea spray on a ship's top levels, was another concern. If too much ice accumulated on the vessel, the *Orion* could become top-heavy and capsize.

Despite the hazards, the ship arrived safely at its destination. By taking the Northwest Passage, it had trimmed its journey by 1,000 miles (1,600 km) and saved $80,000 worth of fuel. The fuel savings translated into a large reduction in the ship's carbon dioxide emissions, adding an environmental benefit to the *Orion*'s list of triumphs.

Earlier that month, another vessel made history by sailing the Northeast Passage, a waterway that links the Atlantic and Pacific Oceans along the Arctic coasts of Europe and Asia. Like the Northwest Passage, it had long been off-limits to shipping. The *Yong Sheng* was the first Chinese merchant ship to successfully use this route. The vessel shaved two weeks off its journey between northeastern China and the Netherlands. In the long run, China could save up to $120 billion per year by using northern sea routes. In China these routes are often optimistically called the "Arctic golden waterway."

RETREATING ICE

The Arctic summer (starting in May and ending around mid-September) always brings a reduction in northern sea ice. With the coming of fall and winter, the ice builds up again. But some of the recent seasonal melts have surpassed all records. The remaining ice covers less area and is much thinner than it used to be. Walt Meier, who investigates glaciers for NASA's Goddard Space Flight Center, describes the steady decrease in graphic terms:

> *In the 1980s, the Arctic sea ice at the end of the summer was about the size of the lower forty-eight states. If you imagine taking a road trip across the sea ice—say you want to go from Los Angeles to New York—you could have driven the whole way. Now you'd reach the ice edge about the middle of Nebraska, so we've lost everything east of the Mississippi [River] and even a bit west of the Mississippi.*

BREAKING THE ICE

Large, powerful, and heavy, an icebreaker features a flat bow (front portion) that allows it to roll up onto the surface of the ice. As the vessel moves forward, its massive weight crushes the ice beneath it. The ship's smooth hull (body) pushes the broken ice farther away. This opens a path for other ships to follow.

A pioneer in icebreaking technology, Russia is the only country in the world with nuclear-powered icebreakers. Unlike a typical diesel-powered icebreaker, which uses 100 tons (91 metric tons) of fuel per day, a nuclear-powered vessel runs on less than half a pound (227 grams) of uranium per day. In 2013 Russia began construction on what will be the largest nuclear icebreaker in the world. The United States, with two operational icebreakers as of 2013, has commissioned plans for four new icebreakers, expected to cost about $850 million each.

The nuclear-powered Russian icebreaker *Yamal* made 47 trips to the North Pole between 2000 and 2013.

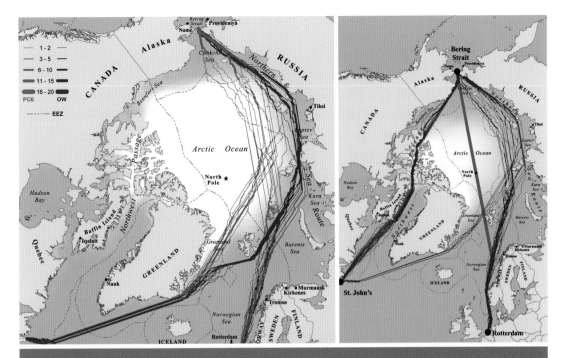

According to computer simulations, Arctic thaw will dramatically increase access to Arctic shipping routes. Compare the number of routes available in 2013 *(left)* to the predicted routes emerging by 2040–2059 *(right)*. Blue lines on the maps show routes accessible to most ships during the summer. Red lines show routes accessible only to ice-hardened vessels.

At this rate, experts estimate that by 2050, ships will be able to navigate most Arctic waterways previously blocked by ice. Equally amazing, they predict the polar ice cap itself may become so thin that icebreakers will be able to sail directly across the North Pole.

For the *Nordic Orion* and the *Yong Sheng*, Arctic waters offered shortcuts to their destinations. But in the eyes of energy companies, the polar region is a destination in its own right. Experts predict that as sea ice retreats farther, shipping traffic will continue to increase. Much of that traffic will come from energy companies aiming to exploit oil and natural reserves. More accessible sea routes will make it easier for drill ships to reach the most promising Arctic waters and for carriers to transport Arctic oil and gas products around the world.

"A DANGEROUS PLACE"

Not everyone is enthusiastic about the prospect of increased Arctic travel. "The Arctic is a dangerous place and always will be," cautions geographer

Laurence Smith. "The ice will always remain in winter. It's dark. It's remote." Because of the hazardous conditions, "the northern countries are going to have some patrolling, search-and-rescue, and security issues on their hands in coming years."

Although much of the sea ice may melt during summer, ships still run the risk of encountering icebergs. In fact, warmer weather increases the likelihood that icebergs will break off from glaciers that extend into the water. An encounter with such an iceberg sank the *Titanic* in 1912. Ships that pass through the newly open Arctic waters will need to take precautions, reinforcing their hulls with steel to absorb any encounters with unexpected ice.

THE ARCTIC'S GREATEST GLACIER

Towering 600 feet (183 m) above the frozen landscape, Sermeq Kujalleq (Southern Glacier) at Ilulissat, Greenland, flows slowly toward the sea like a river of ice. Greenland's glaciers have their source at the enormous ice sheet that covers 80 percent of the island. Gravity forces a glacier to move downhill from the ice sheet. Melted water that seeps through to the bottom of the glacier eases its passage. Huge blocks of ice split from Sermeq Kujalleq and topple into the ocean to become icebergs. Eventually, the icebergs are carried out to sea, endangering ships in the northern Atlantic.

These icebergs calved (split) from the Sermeq Kujalleq glacier in 2007. More icebergs calf from Sermeq Kujalleq than from any other glacier in the Arctic. Each giant iceberg has its own distinct landscape. The largest icebergs loom 200 feet (60 m) in the air, with three times that height submerged in the water.

UNWANTED CARGO

More ships in polar waters will almost certainly affect the Arctic environment. Vessels are likely to harbor unwanted invaders: organisms from elsewhere in the world that will disrupt the existing ecosystems. Insects such as mosquitoes and forest beetles may lurk in the cargo. The larvae of tiny marine animals such as barnacles and mussels could survive by clinging to underwater portions of the vessels.

Ballast water is another gateway for alien invasions. As ships deliver their loads and become lighter, they take on additional weight, often in the form of ballast water, to remain stabilized for the rest of the journey. When more cargo is taken aboard in another area of the world, the ballast water is emptied back into the sea. This water may contain a multitude of nonnative organisms. Newcomers have good odds of surviving in the warming Arctic waters—and they will pose a threat to native species by competing for the region's limited food supply.

"[More shipping traffic is] basically opening up the Arctic region as a huge playground for invasive species," said Lewis Ziska of the US Department of Agriculture. "New . . . biological organisms are going into the area where they have never been seen before. The consequences of that are, quite frankly, completely unknown."

A SMALL BEGINNING

Drawbacks aside, ships are already entering the Arctic. In 2012 forty-six vessels crossed the Arctic Ocean, up from only four ships two years earlier. The number is expected to rise dramatically.

But will all ships be allowed passage? That depends on who owns the waterways. Do they belong to the world? Or can individual countries claim the routes and regulate traffic through their territorial waters? With no straightforward answers to these questions, disputes are already arising.

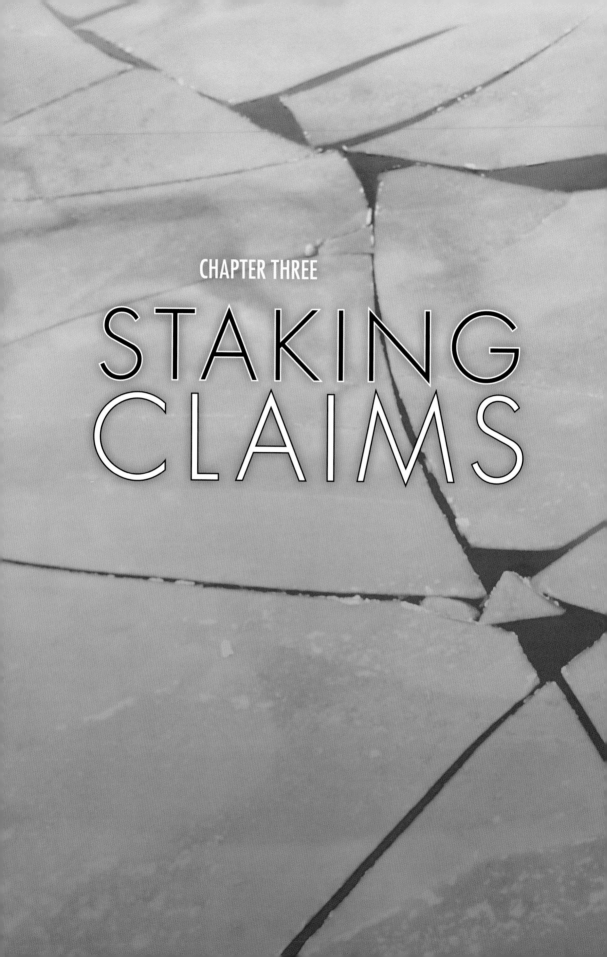

CHAPTER THREE

STAKING CLAIMS

NO ONE OWNS THE NORTH POLE. But if the Canadian government has its way, that could change. In December 2013, Canada submitted a claim to the United Nations for vast stretches of territory in the Atlantic and Pacific Oceans. The area involved is the size of Montana, Idaho, Wyoming, Colorado, Utah, Arizona, New Mexico, and North and South Dakota combined. But that was only the beginning. Canadian scientists are collecting evidence to support a follow-up submission that will include a claim to the North Pole. Putting a holiday spin on the claim's announcement, Chris Alexander, citizenship and immigration minister, issued Canadian passports to Santa Claus and Mrs. Claus. The ceremony was humorous, but the message was clear: the North Pole belongs to Canada.

Canada is not the first country to make such a bold move. In 2001 Russia's government submitted its own official claim to the North Pole— which the United Nations rejected, saying that more evidence was needed. After gathering the necessary data, Russian officials plan to put forward another submission. Denmark also has plans to file a claim for the North Pole sometime in 2014.

"USE IT OR LOSE IT"

Competition for Arctic territory is nothing new. Those quarrels have escalated in recent years. In particular, countries have stepped up their efforts to assert control over waters that allow access to the Arctic. In 2005 a political firestorm erupted when the American submarine *Charlotte* passed beneath the waters of the North Pole. Although the submarine's exact route was not revealed, officials believed it must have passed through Canadian waters. Two years later, in July 2007, Canada announced it was building six to eight navy ships to patrol the Northwest Passage and to protect two military installations in the Arctic. Canada's prime minister, Stephen Harper, said the military bases would "tell the world that Canada has a real, growing, long-term presence in the Arctic. Canada's government understands that the first principle of Arctic sovereignty is use it or lose it, and make no mistake, the government intends to use it."

Canada's position is echoed by Russian officials. "We simply must continue our research of the Arctic Ocean and the Arctic in general," said Russian president Dmitry Medvedev in 2011, "because if we fail to do that, other countries will take control. It's our shores, and it's our sea." The next year, Medvedev's successor, Vladimir Putin, emphasized the point by announcing the construction of several new bases on the Arctic coast to be completed by 2020. Russia has also organized a new Arctic military force and added new nuclear-powered ballistic missile submarines to its Northern Fleet. With this strengthened Arctic presence, the Russian government hopes to assert control over the Northeast Passage, restricting other nations' access to the waterway. Countries will have to apply for permission to use the route and pay for Russian icebreaking services as well as other safety and navigation aids. Russia also seeks to extend its boundaries in the Arctic Sea to claim the oil buried beneath the ocean floor.

But when it comes to officially extending their northern territories, the Russian and Canadian governments must rely not only on a show of force but also on international law. Their most powerful tool is the United Nations Convention on the Law of the Sea (UNCLOS).

THE LAW OF THE SEA

According to long-standing international consensus, a country has the right to control its territorial waters. Until the second half of the twentieth century, those waters extended only 3 miles (5 km) from a nation's coast. But many nations sought to extend the limit as they competed for profitable fishing grounds as well as resources on or under the ocean floor. Governments also worried about water and air pollution from large transport ships and oil tankers. The farther a nation's jurisdiction of its waters extended, the better it could protect and control its coastlines. But how far was too far? Nations rarely agreed on boundaries.

The United Nations responded to the growing number of conflicts through a series of conventions beginning in 1956. At the third convention, which opened in 1973, representatives of more than 160 nations met to hammer out the rights and responsibilities of oceangoing vessels, to establish maritime boundaries, and to protect the marine environment. The resulting treaty became law in 1994, one year after sixty countries had ratified it. Known as the United Nations Convention on the Law of the Sea, it is often called the Law of the Sea Treaty or simply UNCLOS.

UNCLOS established a set of rules that determine how far into the ocean a country can extend its claim. Territorial waters stretch 12 nautical miles from the shore. Nations exercise absolute control over this area. Governments are allowed to patrol a wider contiguous zone—24 nautical miles from the coast—to halt illegal activities, to enforce immigration laws, and to prevent pollution. Beyond the contiguous zone is the exclusive economic zone (EEZ) extending 200 miles (322 km) from a country's coast. No other nation can fish or drill for oil in this region. However, foreign ships may sail through this area.

Nations can push their control even farther by applying for extensions of their continental shelves. The continental shelf is the part of a landmass that lies under the ocean. It also happens to be the most likely location of undiscovered oil and natural gas reserves. According to the US Geological Survey, "The extensive Arctic continental shelves may constitute the geographically largest unexplored prospective area for petroleum remaining on earth." If a nation can prove that its continental shelf stretches beyond the EEZ limit, it receives jurisdiction over the natural resources in the expanded zone, up to 350 nautical miles from the coastal baseline.

By June 2011, 162 countries had ratified the Law of the Sea Treaty. The most notable exception is the United States, where some politicians feel the treaty gives too much power to the United Nations. "No international

> "The EXTENSIVE ARCTIC CONTINENTAL SHELVES may constitute the geographically LARGEST UNEXPLORED PROSPECTIVE AREA for petroleum REMAINING ON EARTH."
>
> —US Geological Survey, 2008

organization owns the seas," Rob Portman, a Republican senator from Ohio, said in 2012. But not all Americans agree with his views. Many US government officials, including President Barack Obama, think the United States should approve UNCLOS. Without ratifying the treaty, the United States cannot file a claim to extend its maritime borders nor can it have any say in the way the Arctic Ocean is divided up. "[The Arctic] could be an enormous area for the United States to protect, explore, or exploit," says Heather Conley of the Washington, DC-based Center for Strategic and International Studies. "But until we ratify that treaty, we will remain on the sidelines."

Even so, the United States is looking for ways to extend its continental shelf into Arctic waters. That was the mission of the American icebreaker *Healy* in 2010. About 500 miles (800 km) from the North Pole, the crew gathered soil samples from an undersea mountain, hoping their findings would support a US claim to the area. One geologist aboard the *Healy* compared the procedure to lowering a thimble from the top of the Empire State Building, then using the scrapings of dirt "to explain the origin and evolution of New York City."

Careful investigation showed that sediments collected by the *Healy* in international Arctic waters matched those found on Alaska's North Slope. This evidence strengthens the case for US ownership of those waters. But the United States cannot file a claim with the United Nations unless Congress ratifies UNCLOS.

ZONE OF COOPERATION OR ZONE OF CONFLICT?

With extremely valuable natural resources and trade routes hanging in the balance, disputes over maritime control in Arctic waters are as serious as they are complex. For instance, the United States and Russia disagree over the maritime border in the Bering and Chukchi Seas. An area of 15,000 square miles (39,000 sq. km) teeming with resources remains in limbo. Another point of contention is the Lomonosov Ridge, which stretches through the Arctic Ocean to the North Pole. Canada, Denmark (through Greenland), and Russia all lay claim to the ridge as part of their bids to secure ownership of the North Pole. The United States maintains that the Lomonosov Ridge is not an extension of any country's continental shelf and belongs to no nation.

PACIFIC OCEAN

Bering
Strait

Alaska
(USA)

CANADA

UNITED
STATES

ARCTIC CIRCLE

Chukchi
Sea

ARCTIC OCEAN

Northern
Sea Route

NORTH
POLE

Kara Sea

RUSSIA

CANADA

Northwest
Passage

GREENLAND
(DENMARK)

FINLAND

ATLANTIC
OCEAN

ICELAND

NORWAY

SWEDEN

UNITED
KINGDOM

DENMARK

Arctic
maritime areas
claimed by

RUSSIA

RUSSIA/DENMARK

DENMARK

CANADA

UNITED STATES

⭐ Military presence

Maritime jurisdiction
boundaries

Sea routes

Nations are building up a military presence in the Arctic to bolster their access to sea routes and their claims to resource-rich underwater territory.

Some observers warn that these standoffs could set the stage for more serious clashes. One concerned expert is US Navy admiral James G. Stavridis, a high-ranking commander with the North American Treaty Organization (NATO), a military alliance of twenty-eight governments. In 2010, discussing the dangers of international rivalry, Stavridis urged "global leaders to take stock, and unify their efforts to ensure the Arctic remains a zone of cooperation—rather than proceed down the icy slope towards a zone of competition, or worse, a zone of conflict."

Few experts expect war to break out over the Arctic. But as nations scramble to increase their presence there, some are taking a distinctly militaristic approach. In 2013 Russia dispatched a convoy of naval vessels on a 2,000-mile (3,219 km) trek through the Arctic. Led by a guided missile cruiser, four nuclear-powered icebreakers followed by ten warships crossed the Northeast Passage to arrive at the New Siberian Islands. On Kotelny Island, the Russian Air Force reopened an abandoned airfield. About 150 troops arrived with vehicles and housing modules to complete the small military base. Along with Tiksi, another base to be reopened, Kotelny Island will monitor increasing traffic through the Northeast Passage. The bases will also guard offshore oil and gas deposits. Plans call for the eventual establishment of a chain of bases along Russia's Arctic coast. Meanwhile, Canada, Denmark, and Norway also defend their waters and proclaim their sovereignty with patrol forces.

CHINA IN THE ARCTIC

China has a different strategy for gaining control over valuable Arctic resources. According to the Law of the Sea Treaty, China has no claim over the Arctic's oil and natural gas reserves. Chinese leaders hope to get around this limitation by helping finance much-needed improvements in other countries' Arctic developments. China can supply funds for roads, deep-sea ports, and search-and-rescue centers. In return for this support, northern governments may allow Chinese companies to invest in offshore oil and to reap profits.

China has already invested $25 billion with two government-owned Russian companies to build an oil pipeline from Siberia to China. In 2013 China paid one of these companies another $60 billion to develop offshore oil fields. That same year, Iceland—hoping to boost its economy through resource development—granted China a license to explore for oil in the

Scientific research expeditions are another means of getting access to the North Pole. China's first Arctic research station opened in 2001 with the flag-raising ceremony shown here. The three-year expedition focused on the study of the region's climate and glaciers.

Arctic. It was an important first step for the country that describes itself as a "near-Arctic state."

US SOVEREIGNTY

In the past, the United States has been less engaged in the Arctic land race than other countries. "[Compared to] the other Arctic nations, we are behind," says Lisa Murkowski, a Republican senator from Alaska, "behind in our thinking, behind in our vision." But signs point to a growing American awareness and interest in Arctic affairs. An Arctic strategy document released in 2013 pledges the United States to protect its security interests, safeguard the environment, and strengthen cooperation between countries. To further these aims, the United States plans to improve satellite communication and establish deep-water ports in the Arctic as well as purchase more icebreakers. US efforts—along with those of Russia, Canada, China, and other nations—will continue to play out on the global stage as the race for resources gains momentum.

CHAPTER FOUR

HIGH HOPES

AND HARSH REALITIES

THE MASSIVE STRUCTURE, CROWNED WITH TOWERS AND DERRICKS, RISES LIKE A FORTRESS FROM THE MIDDLE OF THE SEA.

Prirazlomnaya, Russia's first offshore drilling platform in the Arctic, is built to withstand freezing temperatures, heavy ice loads, and fierce gales. Even violent storms cannot dislodge the 506,000-ton (459,000-metric-ton) facility from the seabed. In December 2013, this gigantic, state-of-the-art platform made history when it began the first commercial production of oil in the Arctic. "We became the pioneers of Russia's Arctic development," announced Alexey Miller, chief executive officer (CEO) of the Russian-based oil and gas company Gazprom. "There is no doubt that Gazprom will continue advancing in the Arctic."

Miller's words are no idle boast. Gazprom has licenses to develop thirty offshore oil and gas fields in the Russian Arctic—a prospect that alarms some conservationists. Greenpeace, an environmental protection group, charges that Gazprom's "safety record on land is appalling. It is impossible to trust them to drill safely in one of the most fragile and beautiful regions

ARCTIC "PIRATES"

In August 2013, two Greenpeace activists attempted to scale Russia's offshore drilling platform Prirazlomnaya. The Russian Coast Guard arrested the climbers as well as the entire crew of their ship, the *Arctic Sunrise*. Everyone was jailed and, at first, charged with piracy. Several months passed before they were finally released.

Russia's extreme reaction provoked outcries across the globe. Analysts believe the harsh treatment the activists received is meant to show the world how fiercely Russia will defend its right to develop Arctic resources. Greenpeace charged that Russian operations lack sufficient procedure and equipment for dealing with oil spills. It claimed that Russian pipelines and wells leak around 30 million barrels of oil products into the environment each year, a figure the Russian government denies.

on Earth." Gazprom officials counter that numerous safety precautions have been set in place to minimize damage to the environment. Still, the challenges of Arctic drilling loom large for all energy companies hoping to tap into northern oil and gas deposits.

OFFSHORE OPPORTUNITIES

As melting sea ice exposes more areas of the Arctic Ocean, massive untapped reserves of fossil fuels may become available for the first time. A 2008 report issued by the US Geological Survey estimated that the polar region may contain as many as 90 billion barrels of oil and 1,600 trillion feet (488 trillion m) of natural gas. About 84 percent of those resources are believed to lie buried beneath the ocean. Offshore drilling stations such as Gazprom's Prirazlomnaya may soon become a common sight in Arctic waters.

Gazprom is by no means the only energy company with Arctic drilling ambitions. Multinational corporations such as Chevron, Rosneft, and Statoil also hold licenses to explore for fossil fuels off the coasts of Canada, Greenland, Norway, and Russia.

US waters near Alaska may hold at least 23 billion barrels of undiscovered oil. But the United States lags behind Russia in exploiting energy resources, partly because development is such a long and costly process.

To gain the right to drill in American waters, energy companies compete against one another in a government-run auction. The companies submit secret bids for the specific blocks of ocean where they hope to search for oil. Winners receive the right to drill exploratory wells, a challenging and risky enterprise. Oil executives must then get approval from numerous organizations before they can begin work. And as Pete Slaiby of Shell Exploration and Production Company notes, "We don't even know if we'll find anything down there in the end."

If the exploratory well does yield oil, the company must secure still more permits from the federal and state governments as well as local authorities. After that, a drilling platform known as an oil rig must be built. A pipeline must be constructed to transport the oil to land. The entire process from the discovery of oil to a producing well usually takes at least ten years.

THE DANGERS OF DRILLING

Even as reduced sea ice makes some aspects of resource development easier, the warming Arctic poses significant obstacles for energy companies. Rising temperatures are melting the permafrost (the layer of frozen soil that underlies much of the land in the Arctic), which causes the ground to shift and sink. This could prove challenging for energy companies hoping to set up drilling equipment, pipelines, and transportation systems on land. Offshore drilling equipment, on the other hand, will be buffeted by shifting ice and powerful waves. Protecting, maintaining, and repairing equipment and facilities in this unpredictable environment will add expense to any undertaking.

On a larger scale, many environmentalists warn of the dangers Arctic drilling poses to the planet as a whole. They feel that a focus on extracting oil and natural gas keeps power companies pointed in the wrong direction when the future should belong to carbon-free energy. "We need a twenty-first century energy revolution based on efficiency and renewables," said Tony Bosworth, an energy campaigner for the

On March 24, 1989, the *Exxon Valdez*, an oil supertanker, ran aground off the southern coast of Alaska and ruptured. Eleven million barrels of oil flowed into Prince William Sound. Damages spread out over 1,300 miles (2,100 km) of coastline. Thousands of animals died. Cleanup efforts cost $2.1 billion and continued over the course of four summers. This photograph, taken on May 3, 1989, shows a worker using a high-pressure hose to clean oil-covered rocks. Many experts fear that a similar spill could occur in Arctic waters, causing even more devastation.

environmental network Friends of the Earth, "not more fossil fuels that will add to climate change."

VENTURES IN AMERICAN WATERS

Executives at Shell are well acquainted with the risks of drilling as well as the costs in time and money. The company first received licenses to drill in Alaskan waters in 2005. Since then it has spent more than $4.5 billion on oil exploration there. After passing all the departmental hurdles, Shell received the go-ahead for actual drilling in 2012.

But problems plagued Shell from the start. Within twenty-four hours, an approaching ice floe 30 miles (48 km) long and 12 miles (19 km) wide put an abrupt stop to preliminary efforts. An explosion followed by a fire rocked the oil rig *Noble Discoverer* while it was in port. The *Kulluk* ran aground on a small island during a violent storm. Although Shell had hoped to dig ten wells during the drilling season, it only began two. With major repairs needed on their ships and equipment, the company announced in February 2013 that it would suspend operations in the Alaskan Arctic for the rest of the year.

Two other oil companies, Statoil and ConocoPhillips, soon announced they too were putting their plans to drill in the American Arctic on hold. Still, Statoil continued to drill in other parts of the Arctic, and Shell has plans to drill off the Russian coastline. As for the future of drilling in American waters, Alaskan senator Lisa Murkowski called Shell's setback "only a pause" in the United States' Arctic resource development. Shell announced in November 2013 that it had presented another version of its Arctic plan of exploration to US government officials. If all goes well, Shell hopes to return to the Arctic in 2014. In any case, the US Department of the Interior is set to consider selling more licenses for oil and gas exploration in 2016 and 2017.

Some lawmakers, however, are skeptical. They believe Shell's past problems show that "even one of the largest companies in the world is no match for the unpredictability, harsh conditions, and heightened potential for human error that characterize the Arctic Ocean." Led by New Jersey congressman Rush Holt, these politicians oppose the possible future auction of drilling rights. They urge a suspension on the sale of new licenses and a reevaluation of existing policy based on "the need to

The drilling platform *Kulluk* ran aground on the southeastern coast of Sitkalidak Island, Alaska, on January 1, 2013. Shell insisted that the newly renovated platform was in prime condition and posed no environmental risk. Other experts fear that drilling in the Arctic could lead to more serious accidents, imperiling fragile Arctic ecosystems.

operate safely, protect the ecosystem, and account for the climate change implications of drilling."

Energy developers and environmentalists alike want safety and acknowledge the need for strong regulations. But even with precautions, the dangers of offshore drilling cannot be completely eliminated. Nonetheless, major energy companies have no intention of scrapping their development plans. "None of the major oil and gas players are going to abandon the Arctic," energy research expert Surya Rajan has predicted. Do the profits outweigh the risks? The answer depends on whom you ask— and may well change as more drilling platforms go into operation.

CHAPTER FIVE

"OURS
IS THE
CHALLENGE"

EDWARD ITTA, A LEADER OF THE INDIGENOUS PEOPLE KNOWN AS THE INUPIAT, vividly remembers growing up without electricity or running water in Alaska's North Slope Borough. The region's remote communities were as poverty-stricken as they were isolated. Schools were few and far between. High school students and even some younger children had to live away from home so that they could attend school regularly.

That began to change after 1968, when the largest oil field in North America was discovered at Prudhoe Bay. Nine years later, in 1977, the Trans-Alaska Pipeline System began transporting this oil south. The United States had a new and abundant source of domestic oil. In turn, Alaska had an equally abundant source of revenue. Every Alaskan citizen received a yearly share of the oil field's profits. New oil-related jobs became available as well. Thanks to the surge of oil money, struggling communities began to transform.

"The first benefit of offshore drilling," Itta notes, "was [the ability] to build schools in every community so that kids would not have to leave their mothers and fathers to get an education." Other advantages soon followed. Health clinics, public works, improved housing, and even small airports flourished in tiny villages and towns.

An oil company support site near Prudhoe Bay, Alaska, is just one of many facilities connected to oil production in the region. Oil-related buildings and equipment cover thousands of acres throughout the state, including its Arctic regions.

After several decades, however, production at the oil fields around Prudhoe Bay dropped to less than one-third of its original output. The slowdown has meant less money for once-poor Inupiat communities that have grown used to a more comfortable lifestyle. Families are once again wondering how they will afford groceries, gas, and warm clothing. Maintaining high-quality schools in the face of declining revenues is especially challenging.

Yet even as Prudhoe Bay's glory days fade to a memory, new energy development projects loom on the horizon. Offshore drilling has the potential to restore Alaska's lost income and give the Inupiat another chance at prosperity. At the same time, though, it could endanger the environment—along with the traditions and even the lives of the area's indigenous people.

Itta, who served as mayor of the North Slope Borough from 2005 to 2011, had no objections to oil wells on land. After all, "Inupiat Eskimos have supported responsible, environmentally sound drilling for the last forty years." But offshore drilling is a riskier proposition, and Itta feared its impact on the Arctic's fragile ecosystems. "We are the Arctic," he explained, "because we are the land, we are the ocean, we are one and the same. That's . . . how our culture has managed to get to this day, through thousands of years in one of the harshest environments."

LIVES ON THE LINE

No one can know exactly what offshore drilling would do to the environment. The process is still too new to offer more than guesses. But indigenous peoples are particularly concerned about the dangers it poses to Arctic wildlife. According to conservationists, the threat begins before an area is even chosen as a drilling site. To determine where oil deposits might be located, researchers conduct seismic surveys. Underwater air guns send sound waves through the water to produce three-dimensional images of the ocean floor. Studying these images helps investigators spot possible oil deposits.

But seismic surveys can confuse fish and sea mammals that depend more on sound than sight to explore their world. Marine scientist Matthew Huelsenbeck elaborated, "Imagine a rocket being launched out of your living room every ten seconds, twenty-four hours a day, for days to weeks

Indigenous whale hunters scout the Chukchi Sea near Barrow, Alaska. Many indigenous hunters use the traditional umiak, a large open boat made of animal skins stretched over a wooden or whalebone frame.

at a time. You could go deaf or be forced to move. That's what it's like for sea life that is subjected to seismic testing, but unlike in people, a deaf whale is a dead whale."

A threat to whales is a threat to the whole Inupiat way of life. For thousands of years, the Inupiat and other Arctic peoples have relied on the whale as a food source. In remote areas where imported foods are often too expensive to afford, whale meat remains crucial to many people's diets. It also serves as an important link to their heritage. By facing hardship and danger during their hunts and giving thanks together for successful expeditions, people forge bonds with one another and with their surroundings. "The whale is central to our culture," explains Itta, a former whaling captain. "It encompasses values such as sharing, spirituality, and being united." If offshore drilling disrupts whale populations, many indigenous people fear these cherished values will be upended as well.

THREATS FROM OIL SPILLS

Once oil is located and drilling begins in earnest, another danger arises: the possibility that an accident on an oil rig will spill tons of oil into Arctic waters. An oil spill is a disaster anywhere it happens. But the Arctic's conditions make a spill an especially likely—and especially devastating—possibility. High winds, icebergs, and lack of sunlight during the winter could easily compromise an operation. If a spill were to occur, these same factors would make it difficult to contain the damage. Whales, seals, fish, and birds may die as they become engulfed with oil or as their food sources are destroyed.

No technology exists to provide a quick fix to an oil spill. While it is hard to clean up oil in more temperate areas, it is almost impossible to contain damage in an icy ocean. Oil that leaks under the ice may stay there for years, causing long-term harm to native wildlife. This devastation of their ancestral homeland is many indigenous people's worst nightmare.

"AN ENDANGERED SPECIES"

Experts agree that it doesn't take an oil spill to place the Arctic environment—and its inhabitants—in jeopardy. Any drilling operations reinforce the world's dependence on fossil fuels, which in turn contributes to the warming of the planet. "Continuing to spew carbon into the atmosphere is only making climate change worse," according to Frances Beinecke, president of the New York–based Natural Resources Defense Council. "The Arctic is where you can see that more clearly than anywhere." Though the consequences of climate change can be felt throughout the globe, many of the harshest impacts will fall on indigenous Arctic peoples.

Alaskan communities are already seeing the results of a warmer Arctic. Houses built on once-firm permafrost have begun to tilt and sag, some dangerously so. Buildings originally above sea level are becoming vulnerable to flooding and storm damage. At the same time, the sea ice that once protected coastal villages from ocean storms is shrinking. With nothing to block the increasingly extreme weather, some land is in danger of being washed away altogether.

Melting sea ice poses other long-term problems. Whale hunters, who must move across floating ice to catch their prey, have trouble camping on thinning ice floes. Other traditional food sources, from caribou to salmon, are also threatened by the changing environmental conditions.

THE VANISHING VILLAGES

The Alaskan village of Newtok is disappearing. The sea ice that once blocked the nearby coastline from ocean storms has dwindled. Without this barrier, fierce waves surge up the Ninglick River, on whose banks the town is situated. The waves are eroding the riverbank at a rate of more than 70 feet (21 m) per year. Newtok's landing stage for barges has already toppled into the water. Meanwhile, melting permafrost is causing the village's land to sink. Some of Newtok's sixty buildings sagged so much that they had to be abandoned.

Experts believe the entire village could be washed away by 2017. Residents hope to relocate the village to safer ground, but plans for a move have repeatedly stalled because of a lack of funds and other resources. Newtok is just one of about 180 Alaskan villages at risk from erosion and shifting permafrost.

Like the village of Newtok, the Alaskan Inupiat village of Shishmaref is threatened by climate change. Ice that once shielded the shoreline from waves is melting, exposing the land to erosion. This home in Shishmaref toppled over in 2006 after the land beneath it was washed away.

If climate change continues unchecked, aided by development of Arctic fossil fuels, these challenges will become ever more pressing. Sheila Watt-Cloutier, former chairperson of the Inuit Circumpolar Council, voices the general anxiety.

> *People worry about the polar bear becoming extinct by 2070 because there will be no ice from which they can hunt seals, but the Inuit face extinction for the same reason and at the same time. . . . We know the planet is melting and with it our vibrant culture, our way of life. We are an endangered species, too.*

Kivalina, an indigenous Alaskan community 80 miles (129 km) above the Arctic Circle, will likely be underwater by 2025. But relocating the village will cost an estimated $400 million. Kivalina's four hundred residents, who live in single-story cabins and depend on hunting and fishing for survival, do not have sufficient community funds to pay for the move. They are looking to the federal government to help cover the cost of relocation, but this aid has yet to materialize. In 2008 residents filed a lawsuit against twenty-four major energy companies—including BP, Shell, Chevron, ExxonMobil and ConocoPhillips—claiming that these companies had contributed to climate change and should compensate Kivalina for the resulting damages. The case was dismissed.

TRADITIONS AND TRADE-OFFS

Although the Inupiat have a strong desire to protect their culture, many feel that at least some offshore drilling is essential if they are to maintain a decent standard of living. Edward Itta cares passionately about protecting the ocean. He also wants his grandchildren to have more than he did when he was growing up. For most of his tenure as mayor of the North Slope Borough, Itta steadfastly opposed offshore drilling. But shortly before he left office in 2011, he reached a science agreement with Shell. The energy company would sponsor research into the Arctic's unique environment to help government and energy officials make responsible decisions as oil drilling becomes a reality in the region. "I think I can rest easy that I have done the very best I could to bring our issues as Inupiat Eskimos to the forefront in a way the oil industry understands," Itta later said.

Caught between tradition and progress, indigenous peoples face a difficult crossroads. As fossil-fuel development progresses in the Arctic, they stand to gain—and lose—more than anyone else. "Ours is the challenge," says Itta, "to protect the land and the water that has always sustained us at the same time we adapt to new uses."

CHAPTER SIX

SPOTLIGHT
ON
GREENLAND

RESIDENTS OF NUUK, GREENLAND, JAMMED THE STREETS LEADING TO THE HARBOR ON JUNE 21, 2009. Some climbed onto rooftops for a better view. A few watched the excitement from the ocean, keeping their kayaks close to shore. They had come to witness a ceremony that would change their country forever.

Queen Margrethe of Denmark presents Josef Motzfeldt, chairman of Greenland's parliament, with the official document expanding Greenland's self-rule in 2009. Greenland's increased powers include more control over natural resource development.

Greenland occupies a unique position among the Arctic nations. For many years, it was a Danish colony. Although it has had its own government since 1979, it is still a territory dependent on Denmark. But on this summer day, eager Greenlanders crowded around to see Denmark's Queen Margrethe II transfer more governing powers to the head of Greenland's parliament.

In honor of the occasion, Queen Margrethe dressed in the traditional outfit of a married Inuit woman: seal fur shorts; tall, red kamiks (sealskin boots); and a colorful beaded shawl. Greenland's prime minister, Kuupik Kleist, hailed the beginning of a new "relationship [with Denmark] based on equality."

"A GLOBAL ROLE"

Under that new relationship with Denmark, Greenland controls its natural resources—including large deposits of offshore oil as well as minerals such as copper, iron, gold, nickel, platinum, and zinc. Greenlanders keep half the income from drilling and mining operations. The other half goes to Denmark. That amount is subtracted from the yearly subsidy (financial aid) that Denmark gives to Greenland.

As the monetary arrangements show, self-government does not mean Greenland is independent. The country has a population of fifty-seven thousand, of whom nearly 90 percent are Inuit. Traditionally, the chief sources of income have been fishing and a small amount of tourism. As of 2009, there were two traffic lights in the entire country. Ingo Hansen, who runs a men's clothing store in Nuuk, told a reporter his hopes that "one day Greenland will be independent—[a goal] I share with many Greenlanders. But our economy has to improve before that can happen."

Most people believe the key to that better economy lies in Greenland's hidden oil and mineral deposits. The largest island in the world, Greenland is covered with a sheet of ice that extends almost 1,000 miles (1,600 km) north to south and 600 miles (965 km) east to west. Almost 2 miles (3 km) thick, this massive body of ice has begun to thaw much faster than scientists predicted. Mining operations that were too difficult, dangerous, and costly in the past have suddenly become more feasible. "I wouldn't mind if the whole ice cap disappears," said Ole Christiansen of NunaMinerals, a Greenlandic mining company. "As it melts, we're seeing new places with very attractive geology."

But as a relatively undeveloped nation, Greenland lacks the capital, technology, and manpower to start large-scale mining. Foreign companies, lured by the possibility of enormous profits, are eager to help. "We are treated so differently than just a few years ago," said politician Jens B. Frederiksen in 2012. "We are aware that it is because we now have something to offer, not because they've suddenly discovered that Inuit are nice people." Aleqa Hammond, who became prime minister in 2013, agrees. "Greenland used to be a big, white blob on the world map. Now we have a global role."

A RARE OPPORTUNITY

As of November 2012, Greenland had granted about 150 licenses for foreign companies to explore for offshore oil, minerals, and rare earths. Rare earths are of particular interest to developers. These metals are commonly used in making electronic devices such as laptops and smartphones. They can also be a major component in fluorescent lightbulbs, batteries for hybrid cars, and even wind turbines. Greenland boasts an enormous amount of these hard-to-find metals, including what may be the largest deposit in the world. Some geologists believe Greenland could supply one-quarter of the world's rare earth needs in the near future. "This is huge," said geologist Eric Sondergaard as he stood on a barren plain believed to hold 10.5 million tons (9.5 million metric tons) of rare earths. "We could be mining this for the next hundred years."

But many people are deeply concerned by the possibility. Rare earths are usually found in connection with the radioactive element uranium. Exposure to uranium can cause genetic defects, certain kinds of cancer, and other serious illnesses. For many years, the governments of Greenland and Denmark, unwilling to risk contaminating the environment, banned the mining of uranium and any other radioactive element.

Because rare earths cannot be extracted without mining some uranium too, those in favor of developing these resources called for an end to the ban. They argued that the economic boost from mining rare earths could help Greenland gain its independence. Ecologists such as Mikkel Myrup, chairperson of a local environmental group, took an opposing view. If radioactive waste pollutes Greenland's inlets and creeks, "we would have problems calling our waters and fish the cleanest in the world," he pointed out.

Debates became heated in October 2013 as Greenland's parliament approached a vote on whether to lift the prohibition. "We cannot live with unemployment and cost of living increases while our economy is at a standstill," Prime Minister Aleqa Hammond declared. "It is therefore necessary that we eliminate zero tolerance toward uranium now." By a narrow margin of 15–14, Greenland's legislative body lifted the ban on mining and exporting uranium.

"SHOULD WE SELL OUR SOULS?"

When mining projects actually get under way, Greenland is sure to undergo many changes. Many Greenlanders continue to worry about what the future may bring. First, there is the overall environmental impact to consider. For example, tankers chugging across the Arctic would release carbon dioxide into the air. This would further the process of climate change and the melting of the Arctic ice. Polar bears and seals, which spend a great deal of time on the ice, could become more endangered than they currently are. In turn, a decline in the bear population would threaten indigenous cultures, which depend on these animals as a food source. At the same time, exhaust from mines could spoil the surrounding landscape, pollute the air, and damage the natural habitats of native species. Sofie Petersen, the Lutheran bishop of Nuuk, said in 2012, "Everyone needs money, but should we sell our souls? What will happen if we are all millionaires, every one of us, and we can't deliver Greenland as we know it to our grandchildren?"

More immediate concerns also plague many Greenlanders. Large numbers of workers from other countries, many from China, are expected to arrive when mining and offshore drilling begin. Some fear that foreign customs and languages could overshadow the Inuit culture. Workers from other countries might take jobs that could have gone to Inuit workers and might gain more political influence than the indigenous population. Well on the road to independence, Greenlanders want to be free to control their own country without undue influence from outsiders.

GREEN ENERGY FROM GLACIERS

Greenland's melting ice sheet provides another precious energy source— vast amounts of water that can be used to generate electricity. Unlike fossil fuels, water is a renewable resource, and hydroelectric power releases no harmful emissions into the atmosphere. By tapping into this form of green energy, Greenland can exploit the Arctic thaw without causing further warming.

September 2013 marked the opening of Greenland's fifth hydroelectric power plant—the first plant in the world to be built beneath permafrost. The facility runs on water that is funneled through a series of tunnels to an underground turbine. The spinning turbine powers a generator that converts the energy of the falling water into enough electricity to power the nearby coastal city of Ilulissat. With the new plant up and running, Greenland's carbon emissions have dropped by 23 percent, and hydroelectric power supplies a record 70 percent of the country's energy needs.

Miiti Lynge, Greenland's minister of housing, nature, and environment, finds the situation deeply meaningful as well as practical. "With green energy from hydropower," he explained, "we use the forces of nature to provide us with electricity, connecting us in a modern way with nature: the power begins as snowfall and [later] the thawing water flows through the turbines."

"WE ARE NOT GIVING UP OUR VALUES"

Despite the island's new political prominence, Greenlanders know they face the same threats from climate change as their Arctic neighbors. Their common task is to balance economic growth with the preservation of the region's pristine environment and the Inuit culture. "We are welcoming companies and countries that are interested in investing in Greenland," said Aleqa Hammond shortly after her election as prime minister. "Greenland should work with countries that have the same values as we have on how human rights should be respected. We are not giving up our values for investors' sake."

LOSING THE ICE SHEET

Two processes are at work as Greenland's ice sheet continues to dwindle. In the first process, rising land temperatures melt the ice. In the second, warming ocean currents erode glaciers that stretch into the ocean. Between these two processes, Greenland has lost an estimated 1,500 gigatons of ice between 2000 and 2008. That's more than 1,500 billion tons (1,360 billion metric tons) of ice!

If Greenland's ice sheet were to melt completely, global sea levels could rise as much as 25 feet (7.5 m), flooding coastal communities and even threatening the existence of entire islands. Scientists believe it could take hundreds of years for the ice to disappear entirely. But polar researcher Jason Box thinks the ice sheet has reached a critical point and "really won't recover unless the climate cools significantly for an extended period of time, which doesn't seem likely."

CHAPTER SEVEN

EXPLORING ALTERNATIVES

THE YOUNG EXPLORERS FROM GREENPEACE FACED A DAUNTING CHALLENGE.

For a week, they had trudged across the ice toward the North Pole, each team member dragging a heavy sled. From time to time, the ice would shift, moving them farther away from their goal. Their supplies were beginning to run out. Bitter winds and temperatures of −22°F (−30°C) hindered their journey.

Greenpeace expedition members lower their time capsule and flag into the Arctic seabed in 2013. During the same week as the team's trip, members of the Arctic Council also visited the North Pole. The Greenpeace activists requested a meeting with council officials to discuss the future of Arctic development and protection. The hoped-for meeting never took place.

Finally, a helicopter from a nearby polar station flew the activists closer to their destination. Numb with cold, they reached the geographic pole on April 15, 2013. This was where the Russians had planted a flag on the ocean floor almost six years earlier. Cutting a hole in the ice, the young people lowered their own titanium flag and a time capsule 2 miles (3 km) to the seabed. The flag had been designed by a thirteen-year-old Sarah Bartrisyia, a Girl Guide from Malaysia. The time capsule contained the signatures of three million people calling for measures to protect the Arctic.

"We're here to say this special area of the Arctic belongs to no person or nation, but is the common heritage of everyone on Earth," said team member Josefina Skerk, an indigenous member of the Sami Parliament in Sweden. "We're asking that this area be declared a global sanctuary, off limits to oil companies and to political posturing."

PROTOCOL AND COMPROMISE

Even as nations scramble to exploit the changing conditions in the Arctic, many also seek to slow the rate of Arctic warming. Can environmental protection go hand in hand with the development of energy resources? Scientists and politicians continue to grapple with the challenge.

In December 1997, after five years of intense discussions among 191 governments, a United Nations agreement was drawn up in Kyoto, Japan. Known as the Kyoto Protocol, the document set goals for industrialized nations to reduce their greenhouse gas emissions by 2012. Fifteen years later, however, little progress had been made. The concentration of greenhouse gases in the air continued to increase. At the 2012 United Nations Climate Change Conference, the Kyoto Protocol was extended through 2020, but many attendees expressed doubt that the goals would be met. "This is not where we wanted to be at the end of the meeting," said Kieren Keke, foreign minister for the Pacific nation of Nauru, warning that the renewed measures will not be enough to stop the "unimaginable impacts" of climate change.

Participants in the UN process will continue to work toward a new, stricter agreement. Meanwhile, individual regions, states, and even cities seek to curb their greenhouse emissions. In the European Union, each industry must abide by a cap on the amount of carbon dioxide emissions it is allowed to produce. If a company cannot stay within its limit, it can purchase credits from another company that met its goal with carbon to spare. New Zealand, the Japanese city of Tokyo, and the state of California also have mechanisms for emissions trading. By curbing emissions, these governments strive to thwart global warming while maintaining an energy edge.

Governments and businesses seeking to lessen their dependence on fossil fuels are increasingly turning to clean energy sources such as wind, hydroelectric, solar, and geothermal power. Electricity generated from these renewable natural sources usually gives off little or no greenhouse gas emissions that will pollute the atmosphere. Clean energy sources cannot completely replace fossil fuels, but they can make significant contributions to the world's energy needs. For a few of these options, there may be no better proving ground than the Arctic.

AN ARCTIC WIND FARM

Many Arctic developers, faced with the challenge of powering machinery in the wilderness, find wind energy an attractive option. Wind farms harvest the power of moving air to make electricity. They work best when spread over a large area so that if the wind slows down in one region, windmills in other locations continue to generate power. Many parts of the Arctic landscape are ideal for this setup.

Determined to reduce its reliance on diesel fuel, the British and Australian company Rio Tinto created a wind farm to help power its diamond mine in northern Canada. Before 2012 the mine used about 185 million gallons (700 million liters) of diesel fuel each year. But most of the year, the area has no reliable roads. Fuel and other supplies must be brought in during a six- to eight-week window each winter when an ice road can be built. The process is expensive, dangerous, and inefficient.

With four 328-foot-high (100-meter) wind turbines, designed to withstand temperatures of –40°F (–40°C), Rio Tinto aims to generate 10 percent of its electricity, cutting its diesel fuel consumption by 1.3 million gallons (5 million liters) per year and greatly reducing its carbon emissions. "If we have a lot of wind, we can shut down some of the diesel generators," says Liezl Van Wyk, the business improvement manager for the mine. Although the prime motive for the wind farm may have been financial, this is a win-win situation. The company taps a valuable resource at the same time it helps protect the Arctic environment.

Norway has begun developing wind power along with hydroelectric power. Kirkenes, Norway, is home to one of the biggest wind farms north of the Arctic Circle. The facility, which opened in 2012, provides power for seven thousand households.

HYDROELECTRIC POWER

Melting ice is another potential source of energy in the Arctic. Greenland has taken the lead in developing hydroelectric power, but other Arctic nations, including Canada, may decide to follow suit. Proposed hydroelectric dams in Canada could supply power to the northern city of Iqaluit, a community of around seven thousand people, as early as 2019. Hydroelectric power also appeals to industries seeking to locate facilities in the Arctic. For example, Alcoa, an American producer of aluminum, is considering constructing hydroelectric dams to collect meltwater and power factories in the polar region.

Although it is generally considered "clean" energy, hydroelectric power can have negative impacts on the environment. Carbon dioxide is emitted during the construction of hydroelectric plants and even during their operation. The creation of a dam may cause flooding in adjacent areas. It can endanger fish by disrupting their habitats. Fish and other aquatic animals can become caught in a turbine and injured or killed by the spinning blades. Nevertheless, the Arctic is likely to see more hydroelectric projects in the coming years.

NUCLEAR POWER ON THE HIGH SEAS

In its quest to bring power to remote, resource-rich Arctic areas, Russia is turning to another form of alternative energy. The frigid waters in and near the Arctic Circle could become home to a family of floating nuclear power plants. The first of these plants, consisting of two nuclear reactors mounted on an enormous barge, is scheduled to begin service in 2016. The reactors will generate enough energy to provide electricity and heating for a city of two hundred thousand people. But the plant's main purpose will be to power gas and oil exploration in the Arctic. The giant Russian energy company Gazprom would likely need power from three to five maritime power plants to complete its goals for Arctic drilling.

Critics, however, have serious concerns about the reliability and safety of Russia's proposed fleet. A nuclear plant generates energy by splitting atoms in radioactive elements such as uranium or plutonium. After they have been used, these substances remain dangerous for thousands of years. To make sure no radioactivity seeps into the environment, nuclear waste is stored in concrete containers at the plant. Despite strict safety regulations, some people fear an accident in which radioactivity is released into the environment.

The shipyard that is building the Russian fleet stands by its construction, maintaining it has met the highest safety standards. But such assurances do not satisfy everyone. "In our country," said Paul Genoa of the Nuclear Energy Institute in Washington, DC, "the Nuclear Regulatory Commission would want to know how a barge tied up at a pier could be defended from potential terrorist attack." Even with risks, however, nuclear power may prove a useful—even necessary—piece of the energy puzzle in the Arctic.

STRIKING A BALANCE

The Arctic's resources—renewable and otherwise—remain a valuable prize all over the world. As the northern ice continues to melt, nations will continue to defend their interests in the region. Some nations, such as Russia and Canada, feel their national identity is tightly bound with the Arctic. Others, such as China, believe the polar region should belong to the world. While countries continue to vie for ownership of the Arctic, energy companies and environmental advocates debate the benefits and dangers of resource development, and indigenous peoples struggle to strike a balance between progress and disaster.

Speaking for residents of the Arctic, Patrick Borbey of the Arctic Council declared, "The people of the north want development, but they don't want to see it at any cost, at any expense." Borbey emphasized the need for ecological and cultural sensitivity in future Arctic energy projects, "so that people can have the benefit of development, but at the same time, we can see sustainable protection of our environment for many, many generations to come."

It is a hope shared by people across the globe.

SOURCE NOTES

7   McKenzie Funk, "Arctic Landgrab," *National Geographic*, May 2009, accessed June 19, 2013, http://ngm.nationalgeographic.com/2009/05/healy/funk-text.

8   C. J. Chivers, "Russians Plant Flag on the Arctic Sea Bed," *New York Times*, August 3, 2007, http://www.nytimes.com/2007/08/03/world/europe/03arctic .html?_r = 0.

8   Ibid.

8   "Russia Plants Undersea Flag in Arctic," *USA Today*, August 3, 2007, http://usatoday30.usatoday.com/news/world/2007-08-03-russia-arctic_N.htm.

8–9 Mike Eckel, Associated Press, "Russia Defends North Pole Flag-Planting," *USA Today*, August 8, 2007, http://usatoday30.usatoday.com/tech/science/2007-08 -08-russia-arctic-flag_N.htm.

9   Gwynn Guilford, "What Is China's Arctic Game Plan?" *Atlantic*, May 2013, accessed June 19, 2013, http://www.theatlantic.com/china/archive/2013/05 /what-is-chinas-arctic-game-plan/275894/.

9   Richard Milne, "China Wins Observer Status in Arctic Council," *Financial Times*, May 15, 2013, http://www.ft.com/intl/cms/s/0/b665723c-bd3e-11e2 -890a-00144feab7de.html#axzz2plB3FPHQ.

12   Seth Borenstein, "Mild 2013 Cuts Arctic a Break, Warming Woes Remain," *Times Herald*, December 12, 2013, http://www.timesherald.com/general -news/20131212/mild-2013-cuts-arctic-a-break-warming-woes-remain.

13   Stephanie McFeeters, "Lynge Talks Future of Inuit People," *Dartmouth*, February 8, 2012, http://thedartmouth.com/2012/02/08/news/lynge-talks -future-of-inuit-people.

13   Shelagh D. Grant, *Polar Imperative: A History of Sovereignty in North America* (Vancouver, BC: Douglas & McIntyre, 2010), 411.

12   "Container Ship's Journey Highlights Prospect, Challenges of Arctic Routes," *Arctic Journal*, September 4, 2013, http://arcticjournal.com/business/container -ship's-journey-highlights-prospect-challenges-arctic-routes.

16   Denise Chow, "Shrinking Arctic Ice Will Lead to Ice Free Summers," *LiveScience*, August 23, 2013, http://www.livescience.com/39147-arctic -sea-ice-melting.html.

17–18 Jennifer Abbasi, "Global Warming Is About to Remake Worldwide Shipping," *CNNMoney*, March 6, 2013, http://tech.fortune.cnn.com/2013/03/06 /global-warming-shipping/.

19   Lisa Palmer, "Melting Ice Will Make Way for More Ships—and More Species Invasions," *Nature*, March 7, 2013, http://www.nature.com/news/melting -arctic-ice-will-make-way-for-more-ships-and-more-species-invasions-1.12566.

23   Vladimir Isachenkov, "'It's Our Shores': Medvedev Pushes Russia's Control of the Arctic," *Toronto Star*, November 11, 2011, http://www.thestar.com/news /world/2011/11/11/its_our_shores_medvedev_pushes_russias_control_of_the _arctic.html.

23   Roger Howard, *The Arctic Gold Rush: The New Race for Tomorrow's Natural Resources*, (London: Continuum, 2009), 63.

23–24 Steve Hargreaves, "U.S. Missing Out on Arctic Land Grab," *CNNMoney*, July 18, 2012, http://money.cnn.com/2012/07/18/news/economy/Arctic-land-grab.

24   Ibid.

24   Bob Reiss, *The Eskimo and the Oil Man: The Battle at the Top of the World for America's Future*, (New York: Business Plus, 2012), 84.

26   Terry Macalister, "Climate Change Could Lead to Arctic Conflict, Warns Senior NATO Commander," *Guardian* (Manchester), October 22, 2012, http://www .theguardian.com/environment/2010/oct/11/nato-conflict-arctic-resources.

26   Gwynn Guilford, "What Is China's Arctic Game Plan?" *Atlantic*, May 2013, accessed June 19, 2013, http://www.theatlantic.com/china/archive/2013/05 /what-is-chinas-arctic-game-plan/275894.

27   Associated Press, "U.S. Lags behind Arctic Nations in Race to Stake Claims to Untapped Resources," *PBS News Hour*, January 2, 2014, http://www.pbs.org /newshour/rundown/2014/01/us-lags-behind-arctic-nations-in-race-to-stake -claims-to-untapped-resources.html.

29   Jake Rudnitsky, "Gazprom Begins Oil Output at Arctic Platform Greenpeace Targeted," *Bloomberg News*, December 20, 2013, http://www.bloomberg.com/ news/2013-12-20/gazprom-begins-oil-output-at-arctic-platform-greenpeace -targeted.html.

29–30 Greenpeace New Zealand, "Gazprom Begins First Production at Arctic 30 Oil Platform," press release, *Scoop World Independent News*, September 21, 2013, http://www.scoop.co.nz/stories/WO1312/S00391/gazprom-begins-first -production-at-arctic-30-oil-platform.htm.

30   Reiss, *The Eskimo and the Oil Man,* 71.

31–32 "What Is Fracking and Why Is It Controversial?" *BBC News UK*, June 27, 2013, http://www.bbc.co.uk/news/uk-14432401.

32   John M. Broder, "With 2 Ships Damaged, Shell Suspends Arctic Drilling," February 27, 2013, http://www.nytimes.com/2013/02/28/business/energy -environment/shell-suspends-arctic-drilling-for-2013.html.

32   "Lawmakers Ask Feds to Freeze Arctic Drilling," *FuelFix*, December 4, 2013, http://fuelfix.com/blog/2013/12/04/lawmakers-ask-feds-to-freeze-arctic-drilling.

32–33 Ibid.

33 Margaret Kriz Hobson, "Offshore Drilling: Is Arctic Oil Exploration Dead in the U.S.?," *E&E Publishing*, July 18, 2013, http://www.eenews.net/stories /1059984582.

35 Edward Itta, conversation with the author, December 11, 2013.

36 Ibid.

36 Paul Vercammen and Thom Patterson, "Alaska Drilling: From 'Hell No!' to 'OK,'" CNN U.S., July 17, 2012, http://www.cnn.com/2012/07/17/us/alaska -offshore-drilling.

36–37 Jim Waymer, "Environmentalists: Oil, Gas Surveys Could Hurt Ocean Life," *USA Today*, April 17, 2013, http://www.bbc.co.uk/news/uk-14432401.

37 Itta, conversation with the author.

38 "Alaska Hunts Oil Amid Arctic Damage from Climate Change," *FuelFix*, October 2, 2013, http://fuelfix.com/blog/2013/10/02/alaska-hunts-oil-as -arctic-damage-shows-most-change-from-climate.

40 Paul Brown, "Global Warming Is Killing Us Too, Say Inuit," *Guardian* (Manchester), December 10, 2003, http://www.theguardian.com/environment /2003/dec/11/weather.climatechange.

41 Vercammen and Patterson, "Alaska Drilling."

41 Reiss, *The Eskimo and the Oil Man*, 271.

43 Sarah Lyall, "Fondly Greenland Loosens Danish Rule," *New York Times*, June 21, 2009, http://www.nytimes.com/2009/06/22/world/europe/22greenland .html?_r = 0.

44 Anthony Johnson, "Greenland: We'll Mine for Our Independence," *Metro*, May 14, 2013, http://www.metro.us/newyork/news/international/2013/05/14 /greenland-well-mine-for-our-independence.

44 Elizabeth Rosenthal, "A Melting Greenland Weighs Perils against Potential," *New York Times*, September 23, 2012, http://www.nytimes.com/2012/09/24 /science/earth/melting-greenland-weighs-perils-against-potential.html.

44 Elizabeth Rosenthal, "Race Is on as Ice Melt Reveals Arctic Treasures," *New York Times*, *CNBC.com*, September 19, 2012, http://www.cnbc.com/id /49087946/print.

44 Alistair Scrutton, "Insight: Great Expectations Fill Greenland as China Eyes Riches," *Reuters*, November 5, 2012, http://www.reuters.com/article/2012 /11/05/us-greenland-idUSBRE8A40MR20121105.

45 Rosenthal, "A Melting Greenland."

45 Johnson, "Greenland."

45 "Greenland Votes to Allow Uranium, Rare Earths Mining," *Reuters*, October 24, 2013, http://www.reuters.com/article/2012/11/05/us-greenland -idUSBRE8A40MR20121105.

46 Tim Folger, "Viking Weather," *National Geographic*, June 2012, accessed June 19, 2013, http://ngm.nationalgeographic.com/print/2010/06/viking-weather /folger-text.

46 "Greenland Powers Up Fifth Hydroelectric Plant," *Arctic Journal*, September 2013, accessed December 30, 2013, http://arcticjournal.com/business/greenland -powers-fifth-hydroelectric-plant.

47 Paul Waldie, "Greenland Rolls Up the Resource Welcome Mat," *Toronto Globe and Mail*, March 13, 2013, http://www.theglobeandmail.com.

47 Suzanne Goldenberg, "Arctic Lost Record Snow and Ice Last Year as Data Shows Changing Climate," *Guardian* (Manchester), December 5, 2012, http:// www.guardian.co.uk/environment/2012/dec/05/arctic-sea-ice-scientists-report.

49 Damian Carrington, "Activists Plant Signed Flag on North Pole Seabed in Arctic Protection Campaign," *Guardian* (Manchester), April 15, 2013, http://www .theguardian.com/environment/2013/apr/15/activists-plant-flag-north-pole -arctic (June 19, 2013).

50 "Climate Talks End with Deal 'Not Where We Wanted to Be,'" *NBC News*, December 8, 2012, http://worldnews.nbcnews.com/_news/2012/12/08 /15777912-climate-talks-end-with-deal-thats-not-where-we-wanted-to-be?lite/.

51 Elizabeth Judd, "Building a Wind Farm in Arctic Conditions: Rio Tinto' Diavik Mine," *Friends of the Wind*, August 4, 2013, http://friendsofwind.ca/building-a -wind-farm-in-arctic-conditions-rio-tintos-diavik-mine/.

53 Patrick J. Kiger, "Russia Floats Plans for Nuclear Power Plants at Sea," *National Geographic Daily News*, October 23, 2013, http://news.nationalgeographic.com /news/energy/2013/10/131023-russia-floating-nuclear-power-plants/.

53 "Interview: China Backs Arctic Agenda of Environment over Development," *English.news.cn*, October 23, 2013, http://news.xinhuanet.com/english/indepth /2013-10/23/c_132824519.htm.

GLOSSARY

carbon dioxide: a colorless, odorless gas that holds heat in the atmosphere and contributes to climate change

climate change: lasting changes in weather patterns, such as increased numbers of severe storms, floods, droughts, and heat waves

contiguous zone: the ocean area extending 24 nautical miles from shore over which a nation has power to prevent illegal activities

continental shelf: the part of a landmass that lies under the ocean and slopes down to the ocean floor, sometimes bounded by an abrupt drop-off known as the shelf break

ecosystem: everything that exists in an environment, including organisms and nonliving elements such as climate, minerals, water, soil, and sunlight

exclusive economic zone (EEZ): an ocean area extending 200 nautical miles from a nation's shore and over which it has sole rights to all economic resources in or under the water

fossil fuel: a substance such as oil, coal, or natural gas that was formed from the remains of prehistoric plants and trees and that gives off carbon dioxide when burned

glacier: a large, slow-moving body of ice

greenhouse gas: a compound, such as carbon dioxide, that traps heat in the atmosphere

iceberg: a mass of ice that breaks off from a glacier and floats out to sea

icebreaker: a massive ship specialized to break through sheets of ocean ice

nuclear power: power generated from energy released by splitting atoms in radioactive substances such as uranium or plutonium

offshore drilling: a process for extracting resources from the seabed

oil rig: an offshore platform from which oil wells can be drilled

permafrost: a hard layer of permanently frozen soil underlying much of the land in the Arctic

pipeline: a long pipe for transporting oil and gas over great distances

radiation: a type of powerful and often dangerous energy produced by radioactive substances and nuclear reactions

rare earths: a group of chemically similar metallic elements such as europium, lanthanum, and promethium, which are found in certain minerals and used in making electronic devices

seismic survey: a study that uses sound waves to make 3-D images of the ocean floor

territorial waters: a zone extending twenty-four nautical miles from a nation's shore and over which it has absolute authority

SELECTED BIBLIOGRAPHY

"Arctic Needs Protection from Resource Rush As Ice Melts: UN Body." *Reuters*, February 18, 2013. http://www.reuters.com/assets/print?aid = USBRE91H0A820130218.

Broder, John M., and Clifford Krauss. "New and Frozen Frontier Awaits Offshore Oil Drilling." *New York Times*, May 23, 2012. http://www.nytimes.com/2012/05/24 /science/earth/shell-arctic-ocean-...to-open-new-oil-frontier.tml:pagewanted = all &_r = 0&pagewanted = print.

Brown, Paul. "Global Warming Is Killing Us Too, Say Inuit." *Guardian* (Manchester), December 10, 2003. http://www.guardian.co.uk/environment/2003/dec/11/weather .climatechange.

Byers, Michael. *Who Owns the Arctic? Understanding Sovereignty Disputes in the North*. Vancouver, BC: Douglas & McIntyre, 2009.

Emmerson, Charles. *The Future History of the Arctic*. New York: Public Affairs, 2010.

Fairhall, David. *Cold Front: Conflict ahead in Arctic Waters*. Berkeley: Counterpoint, 2010.

Grant, Shelagh D. *Polar Imperative: A History of Arctic Sovereignty in North America*. Vancouver, BC: Douglas & McIntyre, 2010.

Hargreaves, Steve. "Oil: Only Part of the Arctic's Massive Resources." *CNNMoney*, July 19, 2012. http://money.cnn.com/2012/07/17/news/economy/Arctic-oil/index .html?iid = HP_LN.

Howard, Roger. *The Arctic Gold Rush: The New Race for Tomorrow's Natural Resources*. London: Continuum, 2009.

Kramer, Andrew E., and Clifford Krauss. "Russia Embraces Offshore Drilling." *New York Times*, February 11, 2011. http://www.nytimes.com/2011/02/16/business /global/16arctic.html?_r = 0&pagewanted = print.

Kramer, Andrew E., and Andrew C. Revkin. "Arctic Shortcut Beckons Shippers as Ice Thaws," *New York Times*, September 10, 2009. http://www.nytimes.com/2009/09 /11/science/earth/11passage.html?_r = 0.

Lord, Nancy. *Early Warming: Crisis and Response in the Climate-Changed North*. Berkeley, CA: Counterpoint, 2011.

Macalister, Terry. "Arctic Resource Wealth Poses Dilemma for Indigenous Communities." *Guardian* (Manchester), July 4, 2011. http://www.theguardian .com/environment/2011/jul/04/arctic-resources-indigenous-communities

———. "Thawing Arctic Opens Up New Shipping Routes on the 'Roof of the World." *Guardian* (Manchester) July 5, 2011. http://www.theguardian.com/environment /2011/jul/05/arctic-shipping-trade-routes/.

"The Melting North." Special report: The Arctic. *Economist*, June 16, 2012. http://www.economist.com/node/21556798.

Palmer, Lisa. "Melting Arctic Ice Will Make Way for More Ships—and More Species Invasions." *Nature*, March 7, 2013. http://www.nature.com/news/melting-arctic-ice-will-make-way-for-more-ships-and-more-species-invasions-1.12566.

Reiss, Bob. *The Eskimo and the Oil Man: The Battle at the Top of the World for America's Future*. New York: Business Plus, 2012.

Sale, Richard, and Eugene Potapov. *The Scramble for the Arctic: Ownership, Exploitation, and Conflict in the Far North*. London: Frances Lincoln, 2010.

Smith, Adam. "Global Warming Reopens the Northeast Passage." *Time*, September 17, 2009. http://www.time.com/time/printout/0,8816,1924410,00.html.

Vidal, John. "Arctic Expert Predicts Final Collapse of Sea Ice within Four Years." *Guardian*, September 17, 2012. http://www.guardian.co.uk/environment/2012/sep/17/arctic-sea-ice/print.

FURTHER INFORMATION

The Arctic
http://arctic.ru/natural-resources
This website features facts, maps, news, and links to videos such as "Putin Discusses the Northern Sea Route" and "The Arctic: New Future."

Arctic Information for Kids: Athropolis
http://www.athropolis.com/links/arctic/htm
This website features a fantasy story set in the Arctic. Numerous links provide a wealth of information on topics such as the tundra, environmental conditions, Greenland, and Arctic history.

Bright, Natalie. *Oil People*. Canyon, TX: Apollo, 2010. Discover what it takes to develop crude oil, from the backbreaking labor of drilling to the precision of seismic survey interpretation.

Climate Kids
http://climatekids.nasa.gov
Follow the links on this NASA website to watch videos, play games, and learn more about weather, energy, carbon, and the ocean.

Johnson, Rebecca L. *Investigating Climate Change: Scientists Search for Answers in a Warming World*. Minneapolis: Twenty-First Century Books, 2009. Join scientists from across the centuries as they unlock the secrets of climate change and its impact on the planet.

National Snow and Ice Data Center
http://nsidc.org/
This website provides updates on the state of Arctic ice, information on climate change, and photographs of frozen regions.

Silverstein, Alvin, Virginia Silverstein, and Laura Silverstein Nunn. *Energy*, Science Concepts, Second Series, Minneapolis: Twenty-First Century Books, 2009. Learn more about the many forms of energy, from nuclear to geothermal, and how they are being used around the world.

Expand learning beyond the printed book. Download free, complementary educational resources for this book from our website, www.lerneresource.com.

INDEX

ABOUT THE AUTHOR

Stephanie Sammartino McPherson wrote her first children's story in college. She enjoyed the process so much that she's never stopped writing. A former teacher and freelance newspaper writer, she has written numerous books and magazine stories. She especially enjoys writing about science and the human interest stories behind major discoveries. Her most recent book is the award-winning *Iceberg, Right Ahead! The Tragedy of the Titanic*, an ALA Notable Children's Book and VOYA Nonfiction Honor book. She and her husband, Richard, live in Virginia but also call California home.

PHOTO ACKNOWLEDGMENTS

The images in this book are used with the permission of: © Slayerspb/Dreamstime.com (backgrounds throughout); AP Photo/Vladimir Chistyakov, p. 8; © ALEXANDER NATRUSKIN/Reuters/Corbis, p. 9; NASA/Goddard Space Flight Center Scientific Visualization Studio, p. 10, © Cary Greisch/Flickr/Getty Images, pp. 12–13; © Sue Flood/The Image Bank/Getty Images, p. 16; Courtesy of Proceedings of the National Academy of Sciences, p. 17; © Patrick Robert/CORBIS, p. 18; © Laura Westlund/Independent Picture Service, p. 25; AP Photo/YUAN MAN, p. 27; © MCT via Getty Images, p. 31; Petty Officer 3rd Class Jonathan Klingenberg/U.S. Coast Guard, p. 33; © Karen Kasmauski/Science Faction/SuperStock, p. 35; © Michael Sewell Visual Pursuit/Getty Images, p. 37; © GABRIEL BOUYS/AFP/Getty Images, p. 39; © Stellar Stock/SuperStock, p. 40; © KELD NAVNTOFT/AFP/Getty Images, p. 43; CHRISTIAN ASLUND/AFP/Getty Images/Newscom, p. 49; © Biosphoto/SuperStock, p. 51; Patrick Kelley/U.S. Coast Guard, pp. 52–53.

Front jacket cover: © zanskar/iStock/Thinkstock;
back cover: Slayerspb/Dreamstime.com.

BOOK CHARGING CARD

Accession No. _____ Call No. _____

Author _____

Borrower's Name